We hope this book has been informative and helpful on your journey to understanding and celebrating older adults. Thank you for your interest and support!

Title: Sports and Leisure-A Celebration of Athletics and Recreation in the Capitals
Subtitle: Venues and Facilities: Iconic and Upcoming

Series: Cosmopolitan Chronicles: Tales of the World's Great Cities
By Kelli Tempest

"The world is a book, and those who do not travel read only one page."
Saint Augustine

"A city is not gauged by its length and width, but by the broadness of its vision and the height of its dreams."
Herb Caen

"The purpose of life is to live it, to taste experience to the utmost, to reach out eagerly and without fear for newer and richer experience."
Eleanor Roosevelt

"The only way to do great work is to love what you do."
Steve Jobs

"Travel makes one modest. You see what a tiny place you occupy in the world."
Gustave Flaubert

"Cities were always like people, showing their varying personalities to the traveler. Depending on the city and on the traveler, there might begin a mutual love, or dislike, friendship, or enmity."

Roman Payne

"The best way to predict the future is to create it."
Abraham Lincoln

"The world is a beautiful book, but of little use to him who cannot read it."
Carlo Goldon

"In every walk with nature, one receives far more than he seeks."
John Muir

Table of Contents

Overview of the book

Sports and Leisure - A Celebration of Athletics and Recreation in the Capitals is a book that explores the fascinating world of sports and recreation in capital cities around the world. From the history of sports in the city to the impact of sports on society and the economy, this book provides a comprehensive overview of how sports and recreation have shaped the cultural and social fabric of capital cities.

Methodology Used to Select the Cities

To ensure a diverse and representative sample of capital cities, we used a rigorous methodology to select the cities featured in this book. We considered various factors such as the city's population, the number of sports teams and facilities, the city's sporting history, and its reputation for hosting major sporting events. Ultimately, we chose cities that exemplify the unique relationship between sports, recreation, and culture.

Chapter 1: History of Sports in the City

In this chapter, we explore the evolution of sports in the city and how it has shaped the cultural and social fabric of the city. We delve into the significant events that have taken place in the city's sporting history and the impact that sports have had on the city's economy and culture. We also highlight some of the notable athletes from the city and their contributions to the world of sports.

Chapter 2: Popular Sports and Teams

This chapter provides an overview of the most popular sports in the city, including the major sports teams and their fan culture and traditions. We explore the facilities available for sports and recreation, such as stadiums, arenas, and parks, and how they have contributed to the city's sporting culture.

Chapter 3: Recreational Activities

In this chapter, we look beyond organized sports and explore the various recreational activities that are available in the city. From hiking trails and outdoor activities to water sports and beach activities, we highlight the many ways in which people in the city stay active and engage in leisure activities. We also look at cultural and artistic events related to recreation and how they contribute to the city's cultural landscape.

Chapter 4: Sports Tourism

This chapter examines the role of sports tourism in the city and the major sporting events and tournaments that the city has hosted. We explore the impact of sports tourism on the economy, the infrastructure and facilities required to host major sporting events, and the legacy of hosting such events.

Chapter 5: Sports Industry and Business

This chapter provides an overview of the sports industry in the city, including major sports-related businesses and organizations, job opportunities in the sports industry, and the challenges and opportunities for businesses in the sports industry. We also explore the various ways in which sports contribute to the city's economy.

Chapter 6: Sports and Society

In this chapter, we examine the impact of sports on society and the role that sports play in promoting social and cultural integration. We explore social issues related to sports, such as race and gender, and how sports-based community development programs are helping to address these issues.

Chapter 7: Future of Sports and Recreation

This chapter looks to the future of sports and recreation in the city, exploring trends and future developments in the field. We also examine the challenges and opportunities that lie ahead and the future plans and initiatives for sports and recreation.

Conclusion

Sports and Leisure - A Celebration of Athletics and Recreation in the Capitals is a comprehensive overview of the relationship between sports, recreation, and capital cities. By exploring the history, culture, and social impact of sports and recreation, this book provides readers with a deep understanding of how sports have shaped the world's capitals. Whether you're a sports enthusiast, a history buff, or simply interested in learning more about the world around you, this book offers something for everyone.

Importance of sports and recreation in capital cities

Sports and recreation are essential elements of modern urban life, and nowhere is this more apparent than in capital cities. These cities are often the epicenter of cultural and economic activities, and sports and recreation are critical components of these activities. In this chapter, we will explore the importance of sports and recreation in capital cities and examine how they contribute to the development of urban areas.

Sports and recreation play a crucial role in the physical and mental well-being of people. Engaging in sports activities helps to maintain a healthy lifestyle, prevent chronic diseases, and promote physical fitness. Capital cities have recognized the importance of sports and recreation and have invested in facilities and programs to promote these activities. As a result, citizens and visitors to these cities have access to world-class sports facilities, parks, and recreational areas that cater to a variety of interests and activities.

Beyond the benefits to individual health and well-being, sports and recreation are essential components of urban development. They have the potential to attract investment, create employment opportunities, and contribute to the overall economic growth of a city. The development of sports facilities and infrastructure, coupled with events and tournaments, can generate significant revenue and create jobs. For instance, the construction of sports stadiums and arenas can create employment opportunities for construction workers, architects, and engineers.

Furthermore, sports and recreation are significant contributors to the tourism industry in capital cities. Visitors from all over the world flock to these cities to witness major sporting events and tournaments, adding to the economic growth of the city. The presence of world-class facilities and events can also attract international sports organizations and create opportunities for collaboration and partnership.

Sports and recreation also have significant social and cultural impacts. They can bring communities together, promote social integration, and foster a sense of identity and pride in a city. Sports events and tournaments create opportunities for people from diverse backgrounds to come together and celebrate their shared interests. Additionally, sports can also be a vehicle for promoting social causes and raising awareness about issues such as gender equality, racial justice, and disability rights.

In summary, sports and recreation are critical components of capital city life. They offer numerous benefits to individuals, contribute to economic development, and promote social and cultural integration. The importance of sports and recreation is recognized globally, and capital cities have invested in the development of facilities, programs, and events to ensure that citizens and visitors have access to world-class sports and recreational activities.

Selecting the cities to feature in this book required a rigorous and thoughtful methodology to ensure that a representative sample was chosen. In this chapter, we will explore the methodology used to select the cities and provide an overview of the criteria that were considered.

The first criterion for selecting the cities was their status as capital cities. Capital cities are often the centers of political and economic power, and they have unique cultural and historical significance. We wanted to focus on cities that represent a diverse range of cultural backgrounds and political systems to provide a broad perspective on sports and recreation in capital cities worldwide.

The second criterion was the popularity of sports and recreational activities in the city. We focused on cities with a rich history of sports and a vibrant culture of recreational activities. This allowed us to explore the different ways that sports and recreation are integrated into the fabric of urban life, and to provide insight into the fan culture, traditions, and facilities that support these activities.

The third criterion was the city's hosting of major sporting events and tournaments. We considered cities that have a track record of hosting significant international sporting events, such as the Olympic Games, FIFA World

Cup, and other major tournaments. This criterion allowed us to examine the impact of sports tourism on the economy of the city, as well as the legacy of hosting these events.

The fourth criterion was the availability of data and information. We wanted to ensure that we had access to comprehensive and reliable information about the history of sports, facilities, events, and recreational activities in each city. This criterion allowed us to produce a well-researched and informative book that provides a comprehensive overview of sports and recreation in each city.

After considering these criteria, we selected the following capital cities for inclusion in this book: London, Paris, Tokyo, Moscow, Washington D.C., Buenos Aires, Canberra, and Nairobi. These cities represent a diverse range of cultural and political backgrounds, and they have unique histories of sports and recreation. We believe that they offer a comprehensive and representative sample of sports and recreation in capital cities worldwide.

In conclusion, the methodology used to select the cities for this book was based on a thoughtful and rigorous process that considered the city's status as a capital city, the popularity of sports and recreational activities, the hosting of major sporting events and tournaments, and the availability of data and information. The selection of the eight capital cities was designed to provide a broad perspective on sports and recreation in capital cities worldwide, and we believe that they offer a comprehensive and representative sample.

Chapter 1: History of Sports in the City
Evolution of sports in the city

The evolution of sports in a city is an important aspect of its history and culture. Sports have been played in cities for thousands of years, and the way in which they have evolved over time can provide insights into the city's social and economic development.

In this chapter, we will explore the evolution of sports in each of the eight capital cities featured in this book. We will examine the different factors that have influenced the development of sports in these cities, including cultural traditions, technological advancements, and the impact of historical events.

London:

London has a long and storied history of sports, dating back to the medieval period. One of the earliest recorded sporting events in London was the annual Shrove Tuesday football match, which was played in the streets of the city from the 12th century onwards. The game was violent and often led to injuries and damage to property, but it was a popular and well-attended event.

In the 16th and 17th centuries, London became a hub of professional sports, with horse racing and prizefighting becoming popular spectator sports. The development of public parks and sports grounds in the 19th century led to a growth in amateur sports, including cricket, football, and rugby.

Paris:

Paris has a rich history of sports, which has been influenced by its unique cultural traditions and social structures. In the 19th century, Paris became the center of the international sporting world, with the establishment of the International Olympic Committee in 1894.

One of the most significant developments in the history of sports in Paris was the construction of the Parc des Princes stadium in 1897. This stadium, which has been the home of the Paris Saint-Germain football club since 1974, is one of the most iconic sporting venues in the world.

Tokyo:

Tokyo has a long history of martial arts, which has influenced the development of sports in the city. One of the most popular martial arts in Tokyo is judo, which was developed in the city in the late 19th century.

The hosting of the 1964 Olympic Games in Tokyo had a significant impact on the development of sports in the city. The construction of new sports facilities, including the Yoyogi National Gymnasium and the Tokyo Olympic

Stadium, helped to modernize the city's sports infrastructure and provided a platform for the development of new sports.

Moscow:

Moscow has a rich history of sports, which has been influenced by its political and social structures. In the Soviet era, sports were seen as a way to promote the ideals of the socialist state, and the government invested heavily in sports facilities and training programs.

One of the most significant events in the history of sports in Moscow was the 1980 Olympic Games, which were hosted by the city. The construction of new sports facilities, including the Luzhniki Stadium and the Olympiyskiy Sports Complex, helped to modernize the city's sports infrastructure and provided a platform for the development of new sports.

Washington D.C.:

Washington D.C. has a rich history of sports, which has been influenced by its political and cultural traditions. The city is home to some of the most iconic sports teams in the United States, including the Washington Redskins (American football) and the Washington Nationals (baseball).

One of the most significant developments in the history of sports in Washington D.C. was the construction of the Robert F. Kennedy Memorial Stadium in 1961. This stadium, which was originally built for American football, has hosted a range of sporting events over the years, including baseball, soccer, and rugby.

Buenos Aires:

Buenos Aires has a rich history of sports, which has been influenced by its cultural traditions and economic development. One of the most popular sports in Buenos Aires is football, which has a long and storied history in the city. The sport was introduced to Argentina in the late 19th century by British immigrants, and it quickly gained popularity among the local population. The first official football match in Argentina was played in Buenos Aires in 1867, and the first football club in the country, Club Atlético Buenos Aires, was founded in the city in 1867. Since then, football has become an integral part of the city's culture, with the local teams such as Boca Juniors and River Plate enjoying a passionate fan following.

Apart from football, Buenos Aires has also seen the rise and fall of various other sports over the years. For example, polo was introduced to the city by British expatriates in the early 20th century, and it quickly became a favorite pastime of the city's elite. The city also hosted the first ever World Cup of basketball in 1950, which was won by Argentina. Tennis, boxing, and rugby are some of the other popular sports in the city, with Buenos Aires having produced many world-class athletes in these disciplines over the years.

The history of sports in any city is shaped by its significant events, which have played a crucial role in developing the local sports culture. In Buenos Aires, there have been many such events that have left a lasting impact on the city's sporting landscape. Here are some of the most significant events in the history of sports in Buenos Aires:

1. 1951 Pan American Games - The Pan American Games, a major international multi-sport event, were held in Buenos Aires in 1951. This was the first time the event was held outside of the United States, and it marked a significant moment for Argentina's emergence as a sports power. The event was a massive success, with more than 2,500 athletes from 21 countries competing in 18 sports.

2. 1978 FIFA World Cup - The 1978 FIFA World Cup was held in Argentina, and Buenos Aires served as one of the host cities for the event. This was a significant moment in the history of Argentine football, as the national team went on to win the tournament, with many of its star players hailing from Buenos Aires. The event also brought a lot of attention to the city, and it helped establish Buenos Aires as a major sports tourism destination.

3. 2001 Copa América - The Copa América is the oldest international football tournament in the world, and it

is considered one of the most prestigious competitions in South America. In 2001, the tournament was held in Colombia and Ecuador, with Buenos Aires serving as the venue for the final. Argentina won the tournament, defeating Mexico 3-0 in the final, in front of a packed crowd at the Estadio Monumental.

4. 2018 Youth Olympic Games - The Youth Olympic Games are an international multi-sport event for athletes aged between 15 and 18. In 2018, the event was held in Buenos Aires, with more than 4,000 athletes from 206 countries competing in 32 sports. This was a significant moment for the city, as it was the first time the Youth Olympic Games were held in South America. The event was a massive success, and it showcased Buenos Aires as a modern, dynamic city with a passion for sports.

5. Argentine Open Polo Championship - Polo is one of the most popular sports in Buenos Aires, and the Argentine Open Polo Championship is considered the most prestigious tournament in the world. The tournament has been held annually since 1893, and it attracts the best polo players and teams from around the world. The final is held at the famous Campo Argentino de Polo in Buenos Aires, and it is a major social event in the city's calendar.

These significant events have played a vital role in shaping the sports culture of Buenos Aires. They have brought international attention to the city, inspired local athletes, and helped establish Buenos Aires as a major player in the world of sports.

Sports have played a significant role in shaping the culture and economy of Buenos Aires. The city's love affair with sports can be traced back to the early 20th century, when football became the most popular sport in the country. The success of the Argentine national football team, along with the victories of popular clubs such as Boca Juniors and River Plate, helped cement the sport's place in the city's cultural identity.

Football has not only shaped the culture of Buenos Aires but also its economy. The sport generates significant revenue from ticket sales, merchandise, and sponsorships. The city's major clubs, Boca Juniors and River Plate, have millions of fans worldwide, making them among the most valuable football clubs in the world. In addition, the city has hosted major international football tournaments such as the FIFA World Cup, which has provided a significant boost to the local economy.

Other sports have also had an impact on Buenos Aires' culture and economy. For example, basketball has a strong following in the city, with the Buenos Aires Basketball League being one of the oldest and most prestigious leagues in the country. The city has also hosted major international basketball events such as the FIBA Americas Championship.

In addition to football and basketball, Buenos Aires has a rich history in other sports such as tennis, rugby, and boxing. The city has hosted major international tournaments in these sports, including the Davis Cup, the Rugby Championship, and the World Boxing Association Championships.

The impact of sports on the city's culture and economy goes beyond just the professional level. Sports play a crucial role in the community, providing a source of entertainment, socialization, and physical activity. Local sports clubs and associations provide opportunities for individuals to participate in sports, regardless of their age or skill level. This helps to foster a sense of community and provides an avenue for social integration.

In conclusion, sports have had a significant impact on the culture and economy of Buenos Aires. Football, in particular, has played a central role in shaping the city's cultural identity and generating revenue for the local economy. However, other sports have also contributed to the city's sports legacy and continue to provide opportunities for community engagement and socialization.

Buenos Aires has produced many notable athletes over the years, who have made significant contributions to the city's sports culture and history. Here are some of the most prominent athletes from Buenos Aires:

1. Diego Maradona - Known as one of the greatest football players of all time, Maradona was born in Buenos Aires in 1960. He played for various football clubs in Argentina, including Boca Juniors and Newell's Old Boys, before making his mark on the international stage with the Argentine national team. He led the team to victory in the 1986 FIFA World Cup and remains a beloved figure in Argentine football.

2. Gabriela Sabatini - Sabatini is a former professional tennis player who was born in Buenos Aires in 1970. She started playing tennis at a young age and went on to win many major tournaments, including the US Open and the Wimbledon Championships. She was inducted into the International Tennis Hall of Fame in 2006.

3. Juan Manuel Fangio - Fangio was a racing driver who was born in Balcarce, a small town near Buenos Aires, in 1911. He won five Formula One World Championships in the 1950s and is considered one of the greatest racing drivers of

all time. He is also the only Argentine driver to win the Argentine Grand Prix, which he won a total of four times.

4. Emanuel Ginóbili - Ginóbili is a retired basketball player who was born in Buenos Aires in 1977. He played professionally for over two decades, including 16 seasons in the NBA with the San Antonio Spurs. He won four NBA championships with the Spurs and was also a key player for the Argentine national basketball team, which won the gold medal at the 2004 Olympic Games in Athens.

5. Luciana Aymar - Aymar is a former field hockey player who was born in Rosario, a city near Buenos Aires, in 1977. She is considered one of the greatest field hockey players of all time and won many major international tournaments with the Argentine national team, including four Olympic medals (two gold and two silver). She retired from professional hockey in 2014.

These athletes, along with many others from Buenos Aires, have not only achieved great success in their respective sports but have also become cultural icons and symbols of the city's sports heritage. Their achievements have inspired generations of young athletes in Buenos Aires and around the world.

When it comes to popular sports in a city, it's important to take into account the local culture, history, and traditions. In some cities, traditional sports like football or baseball have been dominant for decades or even centuries, while in others, newer sports like basketball or hockey have gained popularity more recently.

In many capital cities around the world, football (also known as soccer in some countries) is one of the most popular sports. This is certainly true of cities like Madrid, Paris, and Buenos Aires. Other cities like Tokyo and Seoul have a strong tradition of baseball, while in cities like London and Sydney, cricket and rugby are popular.

In some cases, certain sports teams are particularly beloved by locals and have a strong fan following. For example, in New York City, the Yankees and the Mets are both popular baseball teams, while in Boston, the Red Sox have a devoted fan base. In London, soccer teams like Arsenal, Chelsea, and Tottenham Hotspur have passionate supporters.

It's also worth noting that in some cities, sports that are less well-known globally may be quite popular locally. For example, in Mexico City, lucha libre (a form of professional wrestling) has a dedicated fan following. In Delhi, kabaddi (a contact sport that originated in India) is growing in popularity.

Ultimately, the popularity of sports in a city is influenced by a wide range of factors, including the city's history and culture, the availability of facilities and resources, and the success of local sports teams and athletes.

Description of major sports teams

I. Introduction

- Brief overview of the importance of sports teams in a city's culture and economy

- Introduction to the major sports teams in the city

II. Football/Soccer

- Overview of the history and popularity of football/soccer in the city

- Description of the city's most popular football clubs, including their history, achievements, and fan culture

- Key players from each team and their contributions to the sport and the city

- Discussion of the biggest football events hosted in the city, such as the Superclásico and the Copa Libertadores finals

III. Basketball

- Overview of the history and popularity of basketball in the city

- Description of the city's most popular basketball teams, including their history, achievements, and fan culture

- Key players from each team and their contributions to the sport and the city

- Discussion of the biggest basketball events hosted in the city, such as the Liga Nacional de Básquet and the FIBA Americas Championship

IV. Rugby

- Overview of the history and popularity of rugby in the city

- Description of the city's most popular rugby teams, including their history, achievements, and fan culture

- Key players from each team and their contributions to the sport and the city

- Discussion of the biggest rugby events hosted in the city, such as the Rugby Championship and the Pumas' matches

V. Other sports teams

- Overview of other popular sports teams in the city, such as hockey, volleyball, and handball

- Brief description of each team's history, achievements, and fan culture

VI. Facilities for sports and recreation

- Description of the city's main sports facilities, including stadiums, arenas, and training centers

- Discussion of the infrastructure and resources available for sports teams in the city

- Overview of the city's plans for improving and expanding its sports facilities

VII. Conclusion

- Summary of the major sports teams in the city and their importance to the city's culture and economy

- Implications for the future of sports teams in the city

- Recommendations for further research.

Fan culture and traditions

Fan culture and traditions are an integral part of the sports experience in any city, and Buenos Aires is no exception. The passion and dedication of Argentine sports fans are well known around the world, and this is especially true for football fans in Buenos Aires.

Football matches in Buenos Aires are known for their intense atmosphere, with fans singing and chanting throughout the game, waving flags and banners, and creating an electric energy that can be felt throughout the stadium. Fans of rival teams often engage in friendly banter or heated arguments, and it is not uncommon for the police to be called in to keep the peace.

One unique tradition of Argentine football fans is the use of giant paper mache figures, known as "mascots," which are created to represent the opposing team. These figures are often grotesque or comical, and are displayed in the stands during matches to taunt the opposing fans.

Another important aspect of fan culture in Buenos Aires is the concept of "barra bravas," which are organized groups of fans who support a specific team. These groups are known for their loyalty and dedication to their team, but they have also been associated with violence and criminal activity in the past.

Beyond football, Buenos Aires is also home to fans of basketball, rugby, field hockey, and other sports. Each of these sports has its own unique fan culture and traditions, and fans of all sports take pride in their city and their teams.

In addition to attending matches and games, fans in Buenos Aires also engage with sports culture in other ways, such as through fan clubs, online forums and discussion boards, and social media. Fans often gather to watch matches together in bars and cafes, and there are even organized tours of the city that focus on the history and culture of sports in Buenos Aires.

Overall, fan culture and traditions are an essential component of the sports experience in Buenos Aires, and they contribute to the city's vibrant and dynamic atmosphere.

Facilities for sports and recreation

Facilities for sports and recreation play a crucial role in ensuring that a city can provide its citizens with access to quality infrastructure to enjoy their favorite sports and activities. In this section, we will discuss the various facilities available in the capital cities we have selected for our study.

Football stadiums are an essential part of the sports facilities in many cities. For example, the La Bombonera and the Monumental Stadium in Buenos Aires are two of the most famous football stadiums in the world. They have hosted some of the most memorable matches in football history, including the 1978 FIFA World Cup Final. These stadiums have a capacity of over 60,000 and are also used for other events, such as concerts.

Athletics facilities are also important in many cities. The Olympic Stadium in Berlin, for example, was built for the 1936 Olympic Games and is still used for athletics events today. The stadium has a capacity of over 74,000 and has hosted numerous high-profile events, including the 2006 World Cup Final.

Swimming pools are another popular facility in many cities. The Piscine Georges Hermant in Paris is one of the oldest and most famous swimming pools in the city. The pool is a historic monument and has been renovated several times to maintain its grandeur.

Ice rinks are also a popular facility in many cities, especially in colder regions. The Ericsson Globe in Stockholm is the largest hemispherical building in the world and is a popular venue for ice hockey and other events. The arena has a capacity of over 16,000 and has hosted numerous ice hockey championships.

In addition to these facilities, many cities also have dedicated sports centers that offer a range of sports and recreational activities. These centers typically have facilities for various sports, such as basketball, tennis, volleyball, and others.

Overall, the facilities available in a city play a vital role in promoting sports and recreation among its citizens. By providing quality infrastructure, cities can attract athletes and sports enthusiasts from all over the world and promote a healthy and active lifestyle among their citizens.

Chapter 3: Recreational Activities
Overview of recreational activities in the city

When it comes to recreational activities, every city has something unique to offer. In this chapter, we will explore the different recreational activities that residents and visitors can enjoy in each of the selected capital cities. From parks and hiking trails to cultural and artistic events, each city has something special to offer.

In some cities, parks are the focal point of recreational activities. For example, New York City's Central Park is not only a beautiful green space in the heart of the city but also a popular destination for jogging, cycling, and picnicking. Similarly, London's Hyde Park offers a peaceful oasis for city dwellers and is a great spot for boating, tennis, and horse riding.

Many capital cities are situated near bodies of water, which means that water sports are a popular pastime. In Sydney, for example, residents and visitors can enjoy surfing, sailing, and swimming at famous beaches such as Bondi and Manly. In Bangkok, visitors can take a boat ride along the Chao Phraya River and explore the city's canals, or klongs, which are an essential part of the city's transportation network.

Cultural and artistic events are also an important aspect of recreational activities in many capital cities. For example, Paris is known for its world-class museums such as the Louvre, as well as its music festivals and outdoor concerts. In Berlin, visitors can explore the city's street art scene, which has become a significant attraction in recent years.

Overall, recreational activities in capital cities vary widely, depending on the city's location, climate, and cultural traditions. In the following sections, we will explore some of the most popular recreational activities in each of the selected capital cities.

Parks, hiking trails, and outdoor activities

In many capital cities, green spaces and parks offer a respite from the hustle and bustle of urban life. Parks serve as a place for individuals and families to relax, exercise, and socialize. Buenos Aires is home to many parks, with some of the most notable being the Bosques de Palermo, the Parque Tres de Febrero, and the Parque de la Ciudad. These parks offer a range of activities such as picnicking, jogging, cycling, and boating. The Bosques de Palermo, in particular, is a vast green space that spans over 400 hectares, making it one of the largest parks in Buenos Aires. It features a lake, gardens, and even a golf course.

In addition to parks, Buenos Aires offers numerous hiking trails and outdoor activities. One of the most popular hiking trails in the city is the Reserva Ecológica Costanera Sur, which is a protected natural area that offers a glimpse of the wetlands and wildlife that once thrived along the Rio de la Plata. The trail is well-maintained and offers breathtaking views of the city skyline. Another popular outdoor activity in Buenos Aires is cycling. The city has an extensive network of bike paths that connect various neighborhoods and parks, making it easy for residents and visitors to explore the city on two wheels.

For those seeking a more adventurous outdoor experience, Buenos Aires offers opportunities for rock climbing, kayaking, and even zip-lining. There are several companies that offer guided tours and rentals for these activities, making them accessible to both beginners and experienced adventurers.

Overall, Buenos Aires offers a variety of outdoor recreational activities for people of all ages and interests. Whether it's a leisurely stroll through a park or an adrenaline-pumping zip-line adventure, there's something for everyone in this vibrant and bustling city.

Water sports and beach activities

Water sports and beach activities are popular recreational activities in many capital cities around the world, and the same is true for the cities that were selected for this book. Many of these cities are located near water bodies like oceans, seas, and rivers, which makes them ideal for water sports and beach activities. In this chapter, we will explore the various water sports and beach activities that are available in these cities.

One of the most popular water sports in these cities is surfing. Cities like Sydney, Rio de Janeiro, and Honolulu are known for their excellent surfing conditions and have hosted many international surfing competitions over the years. The beaches in these cities are perfect for surfing, with their long stretches of sand, consistent waves, and warm waters.

Swimming is another popular water activity that is enjoyed by locals and tourists alike. Many of these cities have public pools, as well as natural swimming areas like rivers, lakes, and even waterfalls. In cities like Amsterdam and Stockholm, swimming is a way of life, and many people swim in the city's canals and waterways.

Other popular water sports include kayaking, paddleboarding, and snorkeling. In cities like Vancouver and Auckland, kayaking is a popular way to explore the city's waterways and coastline. Paddleboarding is also growing in popularity, especially in cities like Miami and Rio de Janeiro. Snorkeling is another popular activity, particularly in cities like Honolulu and Sydney, where the waters are teeming with marine life.

When it comes to beach activities, there is no shortage of options. Many of these cities have beautiful beaches that are perfect for sunbathing, swimming, and playing beach volleyball. In Rio de Janeiro, Copacabana Beach is a famous spot for beachgoers, while Bondi Beach in Sydney is popular with surfers and swimmers alike.

Beach sports are also a popular pastime in many of these cities. Beach volleyball is a popular sport that is enjoyed by locals and tourists alike. Cities like Los Angeles and Rio de Janeiro have many beach volleyball courts that are open to the public. In Sydney, beach cricket is a popular beach sport that is played by many locals.

In conclusion, water sports and beach activities are an essential part of the recreational activities that are available in the selected capital cities. These cities offer a wide range of activities for people of all ages, interests, and skill levels. Whether you want to surf, swim, kayak, or simply relax on the beach, these cities have something to offer everyone.

Cultural and artistic events related to recreation

Cultural and artistic events are an integral part of any city's recreational activities, and this is especially true in capital cities. These events provide an opportunity for residents and tourists to engage with the city's cultural heritage while also enjoying recreational activities. Many capital cities around the world offer a wide range of cultural and artistic events related to recreation, such as music festivals, dance performances, art exhibitions, and film screenings.

In some cities, such as Paris and Vienna, classical music concerts are a popular form of cultural recreation. These cities have a long history of nurturing classical music and have some of the world's most renowned concert halls and opera houses. In Vienna, for instance, the Vienna State Opera and the Musikverein are among the most famous concert venues in the world. The city hosts several classical music festivals throughout the year, such as the Vienna Philharmonic Summer Night Concert, the Vienna Mozart Festival, and the Vienna New Year's Concert.

Other cities, such as Berlin and New York, are known for their vibrant contemporary music scenes. Berlin, for example, has a thriving electronic music scene, and the city hosts the annual Berlin Music Week, which brings together international musicians, DJs, and producers. New York, on the other hand, is famous for its jazz and hip-hop scenes, and the city has a rich history of producing some of the world's most influential musicians, from Louis Armstrong to Jay-Z. The city also hosts several music festivals, such as the SummerStage Festival and the Governors Ball Music Festival.

In addition to music, dance is another popular form of cultural and recreational activity in many capital cities. Ballet, modern dance, and traditional folk dances are all popular forms of dance that can be enjoyed in cities around the world. In Moscow, for example, the Bolshoi Ballet is one of the most famous ballet companies in the world, and the city hosts several dance festivals throughout the year. In Mexico City, traditional folk dances such as the Jarabe Tapatio and the Danzon are popular forms of recreational activity, and the city hosts several dance festivals, such as the International Ballet Festival and the Mexico City Dance Festival.

Art exhibitions and film screenings are also popular cultural and recreational activities in many capital cities. Cities such as Paris, London, and New York have some of the world's most famous art museums and galleries, which showcase a wide range of art from different periods and cultures. In addition, these cities host several art fairs and festivals throughout the year, such as Art Basel in Miami and Hong Kong, which attract art collectors and enthusiasts from around the world. Film festivals are also popular cultural and recreational activities in many capital cities. Cities such as Cannes, Venice, and Toronto host some of the most prestigious film festivals in the world, which showcase the latest films from international filmmakers and attract actors, directors, and producers from around the world.

In conclusion, cultural and artistic events related to recreation play an important role in the recreational activities of capital cities. These events provide an opportunity for residents and tourists to engage with the city's cultural heritage while also enjoying recreational activities. From classical music concerts to dance performances, art exhibitions, and film screenings, capital cities offer a wide range of cultural and artistic events that can be enjoyed by people of all ages and backgrounds.

Chapter 4: Sports Tourism
Overview of sports tourism in the city

Sports tourism is a growing industry that combines the excitement of sports events with the opportunity to explore new destinations. Capital cities often serve as major hubs for sports tourism, attracting both local and international visitors who come to experience the thrill of athletic competition, explore new cultures, and engage in recreational activities.

The city's rich sports culture and diverse offerings make it an attractive destination for sports tourists from all over the world. Whether visitors are interested in football, basketball, tennis, or other sports, the city has something to offer. In addition to its world-renowned sports teams and events, the city is also home to a range of recreational activities, cultural attractions, and historical landmarks that make it a unique and unforgettable destination.

One of the most significant events in the city's sports tourism calendar is the annual international football tournament, which attracts top teams from around the world to compete against each other. This event draws huge crowds of both local and international spectators, generating significant revenue for the city's tourism industry. In addition to football, the city also hosts international basketball, tennis, and golf tournaments, among others, which provide further opportunities for sports tourists to engage with the local culture and community.

Sports tourists also have the opportunity to explore the city's vibrant neighborhoods and experience its unique blend of cultural offerings. The city is home to numerous museums, art galleries, and historical landmarks that offer visitors a glimpse into its rich cultural heritage. In addition to cultural attractions, the city is also known for its lively nightlife, with numerous bars, clubs, and restaurants that cater to sports tourists and locals alike.

The city's natural beauty and recreational offerings are also major draws for sports tourists. The city is home to several large parks, hiking trails, and outdoor recreation areas that offer visitors the chance to escape the hustle and bustle of the city and enjoy the great outdoors. Additionally, the city's location on the coast provides numerous opportunities for water sports and beach activities, such as swimming, surfing, and boating.

Overall, the city's combination of sports, culture, and recreational activities makes it an ideal destination for sports tourists looking to explore a new and exciting city. With its diverse offerings and welcoming atmosphere, the city is poised to continue to attract sports tourists from all over the world for years to come.

Major sporting events and tournaments hosted by the city

Major sporting events and tournaments hosted by a city can greatly contribute to its sports tourism industry. In this chapter, we will explore the various major sporting events and tournaments hosted by the city that attract tourists from all over the world.

1. Olympic Games: The Olympic Games are one of the most significant and prestigious international sporting events, with a long history of bringing together athletes from different nations to compete in various sports. Buenos Aires hosted the Summer Youth Olympic Games in 2018, attracting young athletes from over 200 countries.

2. FIFA World Cup: The FIFA World Cup is the most prestigious international football tournament, held every four years. Although Buenos Aires has never hosted a World Cup, Argentina has won the title twice, in 1978 and 1986, which has contributed to the city's sports tourism industry.

3. Davis Cup: The Davis Cup is an international team tennis event that is held annually. Buenos Aires has hosted the Davis Cup Finals twice, in 2008 and 2011. This event attracts a large number of tennis enthusiasts from all over the world.

4. Dakar Rally: The Dakar Rally is an off-road rally raid that has been held annually since 1979. The race was traditionally held in Europe and Africa, but since 2009, it has been held in South America, including in Buenos Aires. The city has served as the starting point for the rally several times, attracting tourists and motorsport enthusiasts from around the world.

5. ATP Buenos Aires: The ATP Buenos Aires is an annual professional men's tennis tournament that is part of the ATP World Tour 250 series. The tournament attracts some of the world's top tennis players and is a major event on the tennis calendar.

6. Buenos Aires Marathon: The Buenos Aires Marathon is an annual long-distance running event that attracts runners from around the world. The marathon features a scenic route that takes runners through some of the city's most iconic landmarks and neighborhoods.

7. Argentine Polo Open: Polo is a popular sport in Argentina, and the Argentine Polo Open is the most important polo tournament in the world. The tournament is held annually in Buenos Aires, and attracts some of the best polo players from around the world, as well as many international polo enthusiasts.

Overall, these major sporting events and tournaments have played a significant role in the development of sports tourism in Buenos Aires, attracting tourists and sports enthusiasts from all over the world, and contributing to the city's economy.

Sports tourism has become an increasingly important sector in the tourism industry, and capital cities have the potential to attract a significant number of sports tourists due to the availability of world-class sporting facilities and events. The economic impact of sports tourism is significant, as it generates revenue for hotels, restaurants, transportation services, and local businesses. In this chapter, we will explore the impact of sports tourism on the economy of the capital cities covered in this book.

Sports events and tournaments hosted by a city can have a significant impact on the local economy, both in terms of direct and indirect spending. Direct spending includes expenditures on accommodation, transportation, tickets, and other related expenses. Indirect spending refers to the impact of tourism on other industries, such as retail, food, and beverage services. The multiplier effect of sports tourism is substantial, with every dollar spent on sports tourism generating additional revenue for the local economy.

The impact of sports tourism on the economy of a city can be measured in terms of job creation, tax revenues, and overall economic growth. The hosting of major sporting events and tournaments can create jobs in the hospitality, transportation, and construction sectors. These jobs are typically temporary but can provide an economic boost for the city during the event. Additionally, sports tourism generates tax revenues for local and national governments through ticket sales, hotel occupancy taxes, and other related taxes.

In addition to the direct economic impact, sports tourism can also contribute to the development of infrastructure and facilities. Cities that are able to attract major sporting events and tournaments often invest in improving their sporting facilities, transportation systems, and other related infrastructure. These investments can have long-lasting benefits for the city, as they improve the quality of life for residents and attract additional visitors in the future.

Finally, sports tourism can also have intangible benefits for the city, such as increased visibility and reputation. By hosting major sporting events and tournaments, a city can gain international exposure and promote its culture, history, and attractions to a global audience. This increased visibility can help attract future tourists and investors to the city, creating a positive feedback loop for economic growth.

In conclusion, sports tourism has become an essential component of the tourism industry, and the hosting of major sporting events and tournaments can have a significant impact on the economy of a city. Capital cities are well-positioned to attract sports tourists due to their world-class facilities and events, and the economic benefits of sports tourism can be substantial. In the following sections, we will explore the major sporting events and tournaments hosted by the capital cities covered in this book and the impact of sports tourism on their respective economies.

Infrastructure and facilities play a crucial role in attracting sports tourists to a city. A city with modern and well-maintained sports infrastructure can attract a higher number of sports tourists than a city that lacks such facilities. In this section, we will discuss the infrastructure and facilities for sports tourism in the city.

Stadiums and Arenas The city has several stadiums and arenas that are suitable for hosting a range of sporting events, from small-scale tournaments to international championships. The Estadio Monumental Antonio Vespucio Liberti, also known as the River Plate Stadium, is one of the most iconic sports venues in the city. It has a seating capacity of over 70,000 and has hosted several international football matches, including the 1978 FIFA World Cup final. Another significant stadium in the city is La Bombonera, the home of Boca Juniors, which has a seating capacity of around 49,000. These stadiums also offer tours to visitors, giving them an opportunity to learn about the history of the venue and the club.

Sports Complexes The city has several sports complexes that cater to a range of sports, including football, tennis, swimming, and athletics. The Buenos Aires Sports Complex, also known as the CeNARD, is one of the most significant sports complexes in the city. It covers an area of over 140 hectares and has facilities for a range of sports, including football, swimming, rowing, and athletics. The Parque Roca, located in the southern part of the city, is another notable sports complex that has facilities for tennis, football, and other sports.

Golf Courses The city has several golf courses that attract golf enthusiasts from around the world. The Buenos Aires Golf Club, located in the suburbs of the city, is one of the oldest and most prestigious golf clubs in Argentina. It has hosted several international tournaments, including the Argentine Open. Other notable golf courses in the city include the Jockey Club Golf Course and the San Andres Golf Club.

Water Sports Facilities The city's location near the Rio de la Plata and the Atlantic Ocean makes it an ideal destination for water sports enthusiasts. The Yacht Club Argentino, located in the northern part of the city, is one of the most significant water sports facilities in the city. It has facilities for sailing, windsurfing, and other water sports. Other notable water sports facilities in the city include the Club de Pescadores, which is primarily a fishing club but also has facilities for water sports such as kayaking and rowing.

Conclusion The city has invested significantly in developing modern and world-class sports infrastructure and facilities to attract sports tourists. The stadiums, sports complexes, golf courses, and water sports facilities in the city offer a range of options for sports enthusiasts to indulge in their favorite activities. The city's location near the water also makes it an ideal destination for water sports enthusiasts. With its modern infrastructure and range of facilities, Buenos Aires is well-positioned to become a leading destination for sports tourism.

Chapter 5: Sports Industry and Business
Overview of the sports industry in the city

Sports have become a significant industry in many capital cities around the world, and Buenos Aires is no exception. The city is home to several professional sports teams, sports-related businesses, and organizations, making it a hub for sports-related activities.

The sports industry in Buenos Aires encompasses a range of sectors, including sports equipment manufacturing, media and broadcasting, sports tourism, and sports medicine. The city has also hosted several international sporting events, which have contributed significantly to the growth of the industry.

The industry has also attracted a considerable number of investors, entrepreneurs, and professionals who are passionate about sports. Buenos Aires has become a hub for sports-related businesses, including sports marketing and advertising, sports event management, and sports media.

The sports industry in Buenos Aires has also contributed significantly to the city's economy. The industry generates revenue from ticket sales, merchandise sales, sponsorships, and broadcasting rights, among others. According to a report by the Ministry of Sports and Tourism, the sports industry contributes about 2% to the city's GDP.

Moreover, the industry has created numerous job opportunities for the locals, including professional athletes, coaches, and support staff, among others. The industry also indirectly supports other businesses, such as hospitality and tourism, through the influx of visitors during major sporting events.

In conclusion, the sports industry in Buenos Aires is a significant contributor to the city's economy and has created numerous job opportunities for the locals. The industry's growth can be attributed to the city's passion for sports, its rich sporting history, and the availability of world-class facilities and infrastructure.

The sports industry in the city is made up of a variety of businesses and organizations that support and promote sports. This includes sports teams, sports facilities, sports media, and sports equipment manufacturers, among others. Some of the major sports-related businesses and organizations in the city are:

1. Sports teams: The city is home to several professional sports teams, including football, basketball, baseball, and hockey teams. These teams generate revenue through ticket sales, merchandise sales, and sponsorship deals.

2. Sports facilities: The city has numerous sports facilities, including stadiums, arenas, and sports complexes. These facilities are used for sports events, as well as for other events such as concerts and conventions.

3. Sports media: The city has a strong sports media presence, including television and radio stations, newspapers, and online sports media outlets. These media outlets cover local sports teams and events, as well as national and international sports news.

4. Sports equipment manufacturers: Several sports equipment manufacturers have headquarters or production facilities in the city. These companies produce a wide range

of sports equipment, including athletic shoes, clothing, and gear.

5. Sports marketing and advertising agencies: Many marketing and advertising agencies in the city specialize in sports marketing, working with sports teams, events, and companies to create promotional campaigns and sponsorships.

6. Sports nonprofit organizations: There are also several nonprofit organizations in the city that focus on promoting youth sports, providing sports programs for underserved communities, and supporting sports-related causes.

These businesses and organizations play a significant role in the city's economy, generating jobs and revenue. They also contribute to the city's reputation as a sports destination, attracting visitors and tourists from around the world.

Job opportunities in the sports industry

The sports industry in any city provides job opportunities to a diverse range of individuals with varying backgrounds and skill sets. In Buenos Aires, the sports industry is no exception, and there are many job opportunities available to people who are interested in working in sports-related fields.

One of the most common job opportunities in the sports industry in Buenos Aires is in sports management. Sports management involves overseeing and coordinating various aspects of sports events, such as marketing, event planning, logistics, and finance. There are many sports management companies in Buenos Aires, such as IMG Argentina and Torneos y Competencias, that offer job opportunities to individuals with relevant qualifications and experience.

Another popular job opportunity in the sports industry in Buenos Aires is in sports media. Sports media involves covering and reporting on various sports events, either through traditional media outlets such as newspapers, television, and radio or through online platforms. There are many media outlets in Buenos Aires that specialize in sports coverage, such as Clarin Deportes and Ole, that offer job opportunities to sports journalists, editors, and other related roles.

Sports coaching is another job opportunity in the sports industry in Buenos Aires. Sports coaches are responsible for training and developing athletes in various sports. There are many sports academies and clubs in Buenos Aires that offer job opportunities to qualified and experienced coaches. Additionally, some coaches may also work with schools or universities to train and develop student athletes.

Sports marketing and advertising are also important components of the sports industry in Buenos Aires. Sports marketing involves promoting sports events and related products and services, while sports advertising involves creating and implementing advertising campaigns that promote sports events or related products and services. There are many advertising agencies in Buenos Aires, such as BBDO Argentina and DDB Argentina, that offer job opportunities in the sports advertising and marketing fields.

Apart from these fields, there are many other job opportunities in the sports industry in Buenos Aires. For example, sports medicine and physical therapy are important fields for individuals interested in working in sports-related healthcare. Additionally, there are job opportunities in sports law, sports psychology, and other related fields.

In conclusion, the sports industry in Buenos Aires offers a wide range of job opportunities to individuals with diverse backgrounds and skill sets. From sports management to coaching, from sports media to advertising, there are many fields within the sports industry where individuals can find fulfilling and rewarding job opportunities. As the sports industry continues to grow in Buenos Aires, there will likely be even more job opportunities available in the future.

Challenges and opportunities for businesses in the sports industry

The sports industry is a multi-billion dollar industry that continues to grow at a rapid pace. As the industry grows, new challenges and opportunities arise for businesses. In this section, we will discuss some of the challenges and opportunities that businesses face in the sports industry.

Challenges:

1. Increasing Competition: One of the biggest challenges for businesses in the sports industry is increasing competition. With the growth of the industry, more and more businesses are entering the market, making it harder for existing businesses to maintain their market share.

2. Changing Consumer Behavior: Another challenge is changing consumer behavior. Consumers are becoming more tech-savvy and demanding, and they expect businesses to provide personalized and convenient services.

3. Economic Uncertainty: The sports industry is heavily influenced by economic conditions, and businesses may face challenges during times of economic uncertainty, such as recessions or pandemics.

4. Pressure to Perform: Businesses in the sports industry face intense pressure to perform and deliver results, whether it's a sports team, a sports equipment manufacturer,

or a sponsor. This pressure can be challenging to manage and may lead to mistakes or missteps.

Opportunities:

1. Globalization: One of the biggest opportunities in the sports industry is globalization. As the industry continues to grow, businesses can expand their reach to new markets around the world, opening up new revenue streams.

2. Technological Advancements: Another opportunity is technological advancements. Businesses can leverage technology to provide innovative and personalized services to consumers, such as online ticket sales, virtual experiences, or personalized training programs.

3. Sponsorship and Partnerships: Businesses can also benefit from sponsorship and partnerships. Partnering with a sports team or athlete can help businesses reach a wider audience and increase brand recognition and loyalty.

4. Diversification: Finally, diversification is another opportunity for businesses in the sports industry. Diversifying into related areas, such as sports medicine, sports science, or sports media, can provide new revenue streams and help businesses adapt to changing market conditions.

Conclusion:

The sports industry presents both challenges and opportunities for businesses. Increasing competition, changing consumer behavior, economic uncertainty, and pressure to perform are some of the challenges that businesses may face. However, globalization, technological advancements, sponsorship and partnerships, and diversification are some of the opportunities that businesses can leverage to grow and succeed in the industry. By understanding these challenges and opportunities, businesses can develop strategies to overcome challenges and capitalize on opportunities, leading to sustained success in the sports industry.

Chapter 6: Sports and Society
Impact of sports on society and community

Sports have been an integral part of human civilization since ancient times. Over the years, sports have evolved, and the role they play in society has also changed. Today, sports are not just about competition, but they are also a tool for promoting social cohesion, physical health, and mental well-being. In this chapter, we will explore the impact of sports on society and the community.

Physical Health and Mental Well-being

One of the primary benefits of sports is physical health. Sports provide individuals with opportunities to engage in physical activities, which are essential for maintaining good health. Regular exercise through sports can prevent chronic illnesses such as heart diseases, diabetes, and obesity. Additionally, physical activity through sports can also improve mental well-being by reducing stress and anxiety.

Social Cohesion

Sports have the power to bring people from diverse backgrounds together. When people engage in sports, they interact with others who share the same interests, creating a sense of community. Sports teams and clubs provide individuals with a platform to connect with others who share their passion, which can lead to lifelong friendships.

Sports also provide opportunities for social integration. In many cities, sports clubs and teams are open to all, regardless of age, gender, or social status. This inclusivity helps to bridge gaps and bring people together. Furthermore, sports can be used as a tool for promoting social inclusion and combating discrimination.

Economic Impact

Sports have a significant impact on the economy of many cities. Sports teams and events generate revenue for local businesses, including hotels, restaurants, and retail stores. The construction of sports facilities and stadiums also creates job opportunities for the community. Additionally, sports events can attract tourists to the city, generating revenue from tourism.

Youth Development

Sports provide an excellent platform for youth development. Engaging in sports teaches young people important life skills such as teamwork, communication, and leadership. Sports can also promote values such as discipline, respect, and fair play, which are essential for personal development.

Furthermore, sports provide an alternative to negative behaviors such as drug abuse and crime. Through sports, young people can channel their energy into positive activities, which can lead to improved academic performance, better health, and overall well-being.

In conclusion, sports have a significant impact on society and the community. They provide a platform for physical activity, social cohesion, economic development, and youth development. Sports are not just about competition but also about promoting positive values, creating a sense of community, and improving quality of life. As such, it is essential to promote and support sports in our cities, as they can have a significant impact on society as a whole.

Social issues related to sports, such as race and gender

Sports have long been considered a unifying force in society, bringing people of different backgrounds together for a common purpose. However, as with any other social institution, sports are not immune to issues of inequality and discrimination. In this section, we will explore some of the social issues related to sports, such as race and gender, and how they affect both athletes and fans.

Race in Sports

Race has been a significant issue in sports since the early 20th century when segregation and discrimination against African Americans were widespread. Despite the integration of sports in the latter half of the century, racial issues still persist in various forms.

One of the most visible examples of racial issues in sports is the lack of diversity among team owners, coaches, and front office staff. Although the majority of athletes in professional sports are people of color, the same cannot be said of the people in positions of power within these organizations. In many cases, this lack of diversity can lead to a lack of understanding and sensitivity towards issues of race and can result in biased decision-making.

Another issue related to race in sports is the perpetuation of racial stereotypes. For example, African American athletes are often portrayed as being naturally gifted and physically dominant, while Asian athletes are stereotyped as being more technically skilled. These stereotypes can be harmful and limiting to individual athletes, as well as contributing to broader societal issues of prejudice and discrimination.

Gender in Sports

Gender is another significant issue in sports, with many sports still being heavily male-dominated. Although there has been some progress towards gender equity in sports, there is still a long way to go.

One of the most significant challenges facing women in sports is the lack of funding and support. Women's sports are often underfunded compared to men's sports, leading to a lack of resources and opportunities for female athletes. Additionally, women's sports are often given less media coverage, leading to less exposure for female athletes and fewer opportunities for sponsorship and endorsement deals.

Another issue related to gender in sports is the perpetuation of gender stereotypes. For example, women are often portrayed as being less physically capable than men, leading to lower expectations and less support for female athletes. Additionally, female athletes are often judged on their appearance rather than their athletic ability, leading to objectification and a focus on superficial qualities rather than athletic achievement.

Conclusion

Sports are an important part of society, providing a source of entertainment, community, and inspiration. However, as with any social institution, sports are not immune to issues of inequality and discrimination. Addressing these issues is crucial to creating a more equitable and just society, both on and off the playing field.

Role of sports in promoting social and cultural integration

Sports have been an important aspect of society since ancient times, providing a means of entertainment, competition, and physical activity. In recent years, there has been growing recognition of the role that sports can play in promoting social and cultural integration. This chapter will explore the ways in which sports can bring people together across social, cultural, and economic boundaries.

Role of Sports in Promoting Social and Cultural Integration:

Sports have the power to bring people from different backgrounds and cultures together. They provide a common ground where people can meet and interact with each other, regardless of their social status, race, gender, or age. In this way, sports can promote social integration by breaking down barriers and creating a sense of community.

One of the most significant ways in which sports can promote social integration is through the creation of opportunities for teamwork and collaboration. Through team sports, individuals learn to work together towards a common goal, fostering a sense of unity and shared purpose. This can be particularly powerful in communities that are otherwise divided by social or cultural differences.

In addition, sports can help to promote cultural integration by providing a platform for the celebration and sharing of diverse cultural traditions. Many sports, such as soccer and basketball, are played and enjoyed by people from all over the world. As such, they offer a unique opportunity for individuals to learn about and appreciate different cultures.

Sports and Gender Equality:

Sports have historically been male-dominated, with women often excluded from participation. However, in recent years, there has been a growing recognition of the importance of gender equality in sports. This has led to increased opportunities for women to participate in a range of sports and has helped to break down gender stereotypes.

In addition to promoting gender equality through participation, sports can also help to challenge gender norms and stereotypes. By showcasing the abilities of women in traditionally male-dominated sports, such as boxing and weightlifting, sports can help to challenge the perception that women are weaker or less capable than men.

Sports and Race Relations:

Sports have also played an important role in the struggle for racial equality. In the United States, for example, sports such as baseball and basketball played an important role in breaking down racial barriers and promoting integration in the 20th century. Today, many professional sports leagues have initiatives aimed at promoting diversity and inclusion, including hiring policies that promote racial equity and programs designed to promote diversity among fans and spectators.

Conclusion:

Sports have the power to bring people together and promote social and cultural integration. By providing opportunities for teamwork, collaboration, and celebration of diverse cultural traditions, sports can help to break down barriers and promote unity. Moreover, sports can be used to challenge gender norms and promote gender equality, as well as to address issues related to race and discrimination. In this way, sports can play an important role in building a more inclusive and equitable society.

Sports-based community development programs

Sports-based community development programs have become increasingly popular in recent years as a way to address social and economic challenges in communities around the world. These programs use sports as a tool to promote social change, build community cohesion, and improve the health and well-being of participants.

There are many different types of sports-based community development programs, each with their own unique focus and goals. Some programs are designed to promote youth development, while others aim to promote gender equality, reduce crime and violence, or address health disparities in underserved communities.

One of the key benefits of sports-based community development programs is that they provide a safe and structured environment for young people to learn important life skills, such as teamwork, communication, and leadership. These programs often involve trained coaches and mentors who serve as positive role models for young people, helping them to build confidence and self-esteem.

In addition to promoting youth development, sports-based community development programs can also help to address social and economic challenges in communities. For example, programs that focus on promoting entrepreneurship and financial literacy can help to create new economic opportunities for participants, while programs that address health disparities can help to reduce healthcare costs and improve the overall health of the community.

One example of a successful sports-based community development program is the Harlem Lacrosse and Leadership program, which was founded in 2011 in Harlem, New York. The program uses lacrosse as a tool to promote academic achievement, leadership development, and social change among underserved youth in Harlem. Since its founding, the program has expanded to serve over 1,000 students in six cities across the United States.

Another example is the Grassroot Soccer program, which uses soccer to promote HIV/AIDS education and prevention among young people in sub-Saharan Africa. The program has reached over 1.5 million young people in 50 countries around the world, and has been recognized for its innovative approach to using sports to address public health challenges.

In addition to these international programs, there are also many sports-based community development programs operating at the local level in communities around the world. These programs may focus on a wide range of issues, from promoting physical activity and healthy lifestyles to building social connections and addressing social and economic inequality.

While sports-based community development programs can be highly effective in promoting social change, they also face a number of challenges. One of the biggest challenges is securing funding and resources to support program operations, including hiring and training coaches, purchasing equipment, and providing transportation for participants. Another challenge is ensuring that programs are accessible and inclusive for all members of the community, regardless of their background or ability.

Despite these challenges, sports-based community development programs continue to play an important role in promoting social change and building stronger, more resilient communities around the world. Through their innovative approach to using sports as a tool for social change, these programs have the potential to make a lasting impact on the lives of individuals and communities alike.

Chapter 7: Future of Sports and Recreation Trends and future developments in sports and recreation

Introduction: The world of sports and recreation is constantly evolving, with new technologies, changing cultural norms, and shifting societal priorities shaping the way we play and stay active. In this chapter, we will explore some of the major trends and future developments in sports and recreation, examining how they may impact our lives and communities in the coming years.

1. Technology in Sports and Recreation Advancements in technology have greatly impacted the world of sports and recreation in recent years, and this trend is likely to continue into the future. Some of the most notable technological developments include:

- Wearable technology: Devices like smart watches, fitness trackers, and heart rate monitors are already widely used by athletes and fitness enthusiasts, but new innovations in this area are likely to emerge, such as more accurate and comprehensive biometric data and advanced tracking capabilities.

- Virtual and augmented reality: These technologies are already being used to enhance the fan experience in sports, but they also have potential for training and competition purposes. For example, virtual reality could be used to simulate real-life game situations, allowing athletes to practice in a safe and controlled environment.

- Smart equipment: From smart basketballs to connected golf clubs, technology is increasingly being integrated into sports equipment. This not only helps athletes track their performance, but also offers coaches and trainers valuable insights into their athletes' training and progress.

2. Sustainable Sports and Recreation As concerns over climate change and sustainability continue to grow, the sports and recreation industry is taking steps to reduce its environmental impact. Some of the ways this is being done include:

- Green facilities: Sports venues are increasingly being designed with sustainability in mind, using features like solar panels, rainwater collection systems, and energy-efficient lighting and HVAC systems.

- Sustainable events: Major sporting events are also making efforts to reduce their environmental impact, such as using compostable food packaging, promoting recycling and waste reduction, and offsetting carbon emissions.

- Eco-friendly equipment: From biodegradable golf balls to recycled yoga mats, sports equipment manufacturers are developing new products with sustainability in mind.

3. Health and Wellness The importance of health and wellness in our daily lives is becoming increasingly recognized, and this is having an impact on the sports and recreation industry as well. Some of the trends in this area include:

- Mind-body activities: Practices like yoga, meditation, and tai chi are growing in popularity, as people seek ways to reduce stress and improve mental health.

- Inclusive fitness: The fitness industry is moving away from a one-size-fits-all approach, with more gyms and fitness centers offering specialized classes and equipment for different body types, abilities, and fitness levels.

- Mental health awareness: Mental health is finally being recognized as an important aspect of overall health and wellness, and sports and recreation activities are increasingly being used to promote mental well-being.

4. E-Sports and Online Recreation The rise of online gaming and e-sports has created new opportunities for people to engage with sports and recreation in a virtual environment. Some of the trends in this area include:

- E-sports tournaments: E-sports competitions are becoming more popular and lucrative, with major events drawing huge audiences and offering significant prize money.

- Virtual fitness classes: With the rise of online fitness platforms, people can now participate in group fitness classes from the comfort of their own homes.

- Augmented reality gaming: Mobile games like Pokemon Go have popularized augmented reality gaming, which combines virtual elements with real-world environments. This technology could be used to create new types of sports and recreation experiences in the future.

Conclusion: The world of sports and recreation is constantly evolving, and these are just a few of the trends and developments we can expect to see in the coming years. By staying abreast of these changes, we can better prepare ourselves and our communities for a future where sports and recreation play an even greater role in our lives. One trend that is already becoming more prominent is the use of technology in sports and recreation. From wearable devices that track our physical activity to virtual reality systems that allow us to experience sports in new ways, technology is transforming the way we play and watch sports. Another trend is the growing importance of sustainability and environmentally-friendly practices in sports and recreation, such as the use of eco-friendly materials in equipment and the adoption of sustainable practices in the construction and management of sports facilities. Additionally, we can expect to see a continued emphasis on inclusivity and diversity in sports, as more organizations and communities work to ensure that everyone has access to and feels welcome in sports and recreation. As we look to the future, it is clear that sports and recreation will continue to bring people together, promote health and well-being, and provide opportunities for growth and development.

Challenges and opportunities for sports and recreation in the city

The city has always been a hub for sports and recreational activities, with a multitude of options available for both residents and visitors. However, as the city grows and evolves, so do the challenges and opportunities that arise in the realm of sports and recreation.

One of the main challenges facing sports and recreation in the city is the issue of funding. As the cost of living rises and the city's budget becomes increasingly stretched, funding for sports and recreational programs may become scarce. This could result in a lack of resources and support for local sports teams and organizations, as well as a reduction in the availability of recreational facilities and programs for the community.

Another challenge facing sports and recreation in the city is the need for inclusivity and accessibility. In order to truly thrive, sports and recreational programs need to be accessible to everyone, regardless of their age, gender, race, or socioeconomic status. This requires a concerted effort to ensure that facilities are ADA compliant, programs are culturally sensitive and inclusive, and opportunities for participation are available to all.

Despite these challenges, there are also many opportunities for the future of sports and recreation in the city. One major opportunity is the potential for increased investment in sports tourism. As the city becomes more well-known for its sports and recreational offerings, it has the potential to attract more tourists and generate additional revenue.

Another opportunity for sports and recreation in the city is the use of technology to enhance the participant experience. From wearable technology to virtual reality training programs, there are many ways that technology can be used to improve the quality of sports and recreational programs and make them more engaging and accessible.

In addition, the city has the opportunity to build on its existing strengths and continue to develop new offerings in the world of sports and recreation. With a wide range of facilities and programs already in place, the city has the potential to become a leader in a variety of sports and recreational activities, from e-sports to extreme sports.

Overall, the challenges and opportunities facing sports and recreation in the city are diverse and complex. However, with a commitment to inclusivity, accessibility, and innovation, there is no doubt that the city can continue to thrive as a hub for sports and recreational activities for years to come.

Future plans and initiatives for sports and recreation

As cities around the world continue to recognize the important role that sports and recreation play in the physical and social well-being of their citizens, many are developing ambitious plans and initiatives to enhance and expand these offerings in their communities. In this section, we will explore some of the future plans and initiatives for sports and recreation in our city.

1. New Facilities and Infrastructure One of the most significant ways that cities are investing in sports and recreation is by building new facilities and infrastructure. This includes not only traditional sports venues like stadiums and arenas but also parks, trails, and other outdoor recreational spaces. In our city, plans are already underway to build several new facilities, including a state-of-the-art soccer complex and a multi-use indoor sports and entertainment arena.

2. Technology and Innovation Advancements in technology are rapidly transforming the world of sports and recreation, and cities are taking notice. From virtual reality training programs to smart fitness equipment, technology is enabling athletes and fitness enthusiasts to take their performance to the next level. Our city is exploring ways to

incorporate more technology and innovation into our sports and recreation offerings, including the use of sensors and other devices to track performance and improve safety.

3. Inclusivity and Diversity As we discussed earlier in this chapter, issues of inclusivity and diversity are becoming increasingly important in the world of sports and recreation. Many cities are taking proactive steps to ensure that their offerings are accessible and welcoming to people of all backgrounds and abilities. In our city, this includes initiatives like offering adaptive sports programs for individuals with disabilities and working to make our sports facilities more accessible to everyone.

4. Sustainability With concerns over climate change and environmental impact on the rise, many cities are exploring ways to make their sports and recreation offerings more sustainable. This includes everything from building green facilities to promoting eco-friendly modes of transportation to and from sports events. In our city, plans are in place to develop a comprehensive sustainability plan for our sports and recreation offerings, with a goal of becoming a leader in environmentally responsible sports and recreation practices.

5. Partnerships and Collaborations Finally, as the world of sports and recreation becomes increasingly complex

and interconnected, cities are recognizing the importance of partnerships and collaborations in achieving their goals. This includes working closely with local sports teams and organizations, as well as collaborating with businesses, non-profits, and other stakeholders to develop innovative and impactful programs and initiatives. In our city, partnerships and collaborations are already underway to help advance our sports and recreation offerings and ensure that they continue to meet the needs of our diverse community.

In conclusion, the future of sports and recreation in our city is bright, with exciting new facilities, innovative technology, and a strong commitment to inclusivity, sustainability, and collaboration. By continuing to invest in these areas, we can help ensure that sports and recreation continue to play an important role in the physical and social well-being of our community for years to come.

Conclusion
Summary of key points

The world of sports and recreation is vast, and in this report, we have explored various aspects of it in the context of a city. From the history and evolution of sports in the city to its current state and future prospects, we have covered a lot of ground. Here, we summarize the key points we have discussed in this report.

In the first chapter, we learned about the history of sports in the city and how it has evolved over time. We saw how sports have always been an integral part of human society and how they have undergone significant changes to become what we see today. We also learned about the various factors that have contributed to the growth of sports in the city.

In the second chapter, we explored the role of sports in promoting health and wellness. We saw how sports can help people maintain a healthy lifestyle and prevent various diseases. We also discussed the benefits of physical activity and the importance of encouraging people to participate in sports and other physical activities.

In the third chapter, we looked at various recreational activities available in the city. We saw how these activities provide people with an opportunity to relax and have fun, and we discussed the various water sports and beach activities available in the city. We also talked about cultural and artistic events related to recreation.

In the fourth chapter, we discussed sports tourism in the city. We explored the major sporting events and tournaments hosted by the city and their impact on the local economy. We also looked at the infrastructure and facilities available for sports tourism in the city.

In the fifth chapter, we examined the sports industry and business in the city. We saw the various sports-related businesses and organizations operating in the city, and we discussed the job opportunities available in the sports industry. We also explored the challenges and opportunities for businesses in the sports industry.

In the sixth chapter, we explored the impact of sports on society and community. We saw how sports can promote social and cultural integration, and we discussed social issues related to sports, such as race and gender. We also looked at sports-based community development programs.

In the seventh and final chapter, we looked at the future of sports and recreation in the city. We discussed various trends and future developments in sports and recreation, and we explored the challenges and opportunities for sports and recreation in the city. We also talked about future plans and initiatives for sports and recreation in the city.

In conclusion, this report has provided a comprehensive overview of the world of sports and recreation in a city. We have explored various aspects of it, from its history and evolution to its current state and future prospects. We have seen how sports and recreation play a crucial role in promoting health and wellness, promoting social and cultural integration, and boosting the local economy. By understanding the importance of sports and recreation and staying abreast of the latest trends and developments, we can prepare ourselves and our communities for a future where sports and recreation continue to play a significant role.

Implications for the future

As we conclude this comprehensive study on sports and recreation in the city, it is important to reflect on the implications of the findings for the future. The study has revealed the significant impact of sports and recreation on various aspects of the city, including the economy, social and cultural integration, community development, and individual well-being. This impact is expected to continue and even grow in the future.

One implication for the future is the need for continued investment in sports and recreation infrastructure and facilities. As the city continues to grow, so will the demand for sports and recreational activities. Therefore, there will be a need for more and better facilities to meet this demand. This includes not only traditional sports venues but also parks, playgrounds, and other recreational spaces that encourage physical activity.

Another implication is the need for ongoing efforts to address social issues related to sports, such as race and gender. Despite progress in recent years, there is still much work to be done to ensure equity and inclusion in sports and recreation. This includes promoting diversity in leadership positions, addressing barriers to participation for marginalized groups, and addressing issues of discrimination and bias.

Furthermore, the study has revealed the potential for sports and recreation to be leveraged as a tool for community development and social integration. This implies the need for continued investment in sports-based community development programs, which have proven effective in promoting social cohesion and individual well-being.

Finally, the study has highlighted the need for continued research and monitoring of trends and developments in sports and recreation. The world of sports and recreation is constantly evolving, and it is essential to stay abreast of these changes to ensure that the city remains competitive and responsive to the needs and preferences of its residents.

In conclusion, this study has demonstrated the vital role of sports and recreation in the city, not only as a source of entertainment but also as a catalyst for economic growth, social and cultural integration, community development, and individual well-being. The findings provide valuable insights and implications for the future, which should be considered by policymakers, stakeholders, and residents alike. By continuing to invest in sports and recreation, addressing social issues, and monitoring trends and developments, the city can ensure a bright and active future for all its residents.

As the world of sports and recreation continues to evolve, there are numerous areas where further research is needed to better understand the implications and opportunities for the future. Here are a few key recommendations for further research:

1. Impact of technology on sports and recreation: With the increasing use of technology in sports, including virtual and augmented reality, there is a need for research to understand how these advancements will impact the future of sports and recreation.

2. Social issues in sports: There is a need for further research on the intersection of sports and social issues such as race, gender, and sexuality. This research can help to inform policies and practices that promote inclusivity and diversity in sports.

3. Economic impact of sports tourism: While the economic impact of sports tourism is well documented, further research is needed to understand the long-term sustainability and benefits for host communities.

4. Health and well-being benefits of sports and recreation: Research has shown that participating in sports and recreation can have numerous health and well-being benefits. However, there is a need for further research to

better understand the specific types of sports and recreation activities that have the greatest impact on health outcomes.

5. Environmental sustainability in sports: As concerns about climate change and environmental sustainability grow, there is a need for further research on the impact of sports and recreation on the environment, as well as strategies for promoting sustainability in sports.

By addressing these research gaps, we can better understand the implications and opportunities for the future of sports and recreation, and make informed decisions that benefit both individuals and communities.

THE END

Key Terms and Definitions

To help you better understand the language and concepts related to aging and older adults, below you will find a list of key terms and their definitions.

1. Sports Tourism: The act of traveling to a destination for the purpose of participating in or watching a sporting event.

2. Sports Industry: The business of producing, promoting, and organizing sports and sporting events.

3. Community Development: A process where community members come together to identify and take collective action on common problems, needs, and opportunities.

4. Infrastructure: The basic physical and organizational structures and facilities (e.g. buildings, roads, and power supplies) needed for the operation of a society or enterprise.

5. Recreation: Activities that are done for enjoyment during leisure time.

6. Social Integration: The process of creating a sense of community and belonging among people from different cultural, ethnic, and socio-economic backgrounds.

7. Sustainability: Meeting the needs of the present without compromising the ability of future generations to meet their own needs.

8. Event Management: The process of planning, organizing, and executing an event, such as a sporting event or tournament.

9. Economic Impact: The effect that a particular event or activity has on the economy of a region or country.

10. Diversity: The range of differences that exist among people, including differences in race, ethnicity, gender, sexual orientation, and socio-economic status.

Supporting Materials

Introduction:

- Gibson, H. (2015). Sports tourism: Concepts and theories. In Routledge Handbook of Sports Tourism (pp. 11-21). Routledge.

- Higham, J., & Hinch, T. (2018). Sport tourism development (2nd ed.). Channel View Publications.

Chapter 1: History of Sports in the City

- Harris, C. R. (2019). Detroit's sports history: 1800s to the present. Arcadia Publishing.

- Lentz, G. W. (2015). Detroit: A sports history. Arcadia Publishing.

Chapter 2: Popular Sports and Teams

- Newman, M. J., & Giardina, M. D. (Eds.). (2012). Sports in American history: From colonization to globalization (Vol. 1). Human Kinetics.

- Pasternack, B. A., & Bailey, J. S. (Eds.). (2018). Major League sports and the Americanization of Canada. University of British Columbia Press.

Chapter 3: Recreational Activities

- Jackson, E. L. (2016). The impact of parks on property values: A review of the empirical evidence. Journal of Planning Literature, 31(4), 383-394.

- Kaczynski, A. T., & Henderson, K. A. (2007). Environmental correlates of physical activity: A review of evidence about parks and recreation. Leisure Sciences, 29(4), 315-354.

Chapter 4: Sports Tourism

- Ali-Knight, J., Robertson, M., Fyall, A., & Ladkin, A. (Eds.). (2012). International perspectives of festivals and events: Paradigms of analysis. Routledge.
- Hall, C. M., & Page, S. J. (2014). The geography of tourism and recreation: Environment, place and space (4th ed.). Routledge.

Chapter 5: Sports Industry and Business

- Ferkins, L., Shilbury, D., & van Leeuwen, L. (2016). Managing sport business: An introduction. Routledge.
- Gratton, C., & Jones, I. (Eds.). (2010). Research methods for sport studies and sport management: A practical guide. Routledge.

Chapter 6: Sports and Society

- Coakley, J., & Pike, E. (2017). Sports in society: Issues and controversies (12th ed.). McGraw-Hill Education.
- Lyras, A., & Welty Peachey, J. (Eds.). (2011). Research methods and design in sport management. Human Kinetics.

Chapter 7: Future of Sports and Recreation

- Frawley, S., & Adair, D. (2018). The future of sport management. Routledge.

- Hums, M. A., & MacLean, J. C. (Eds.). (2017). Contemporary sport management (6th ed.). Human Kinetics.

Conclusion:

- Gibson, H. (2015). Sport tourism: Concepts and theories. In Routledge Handbook of Sports Tourism (pp. 11-21). Routledge.

- Higham, J., & Hinch, T. (2018). Sport tourism development (2nd ed.). Channel View Publications.